THE FARMINGTON LIBRARY

350 BOOKS FOR 350 YEARS
1640-1990

GIVEN BY

THE MARTIN KIBBE

FAMILY

SAILING SHIPS

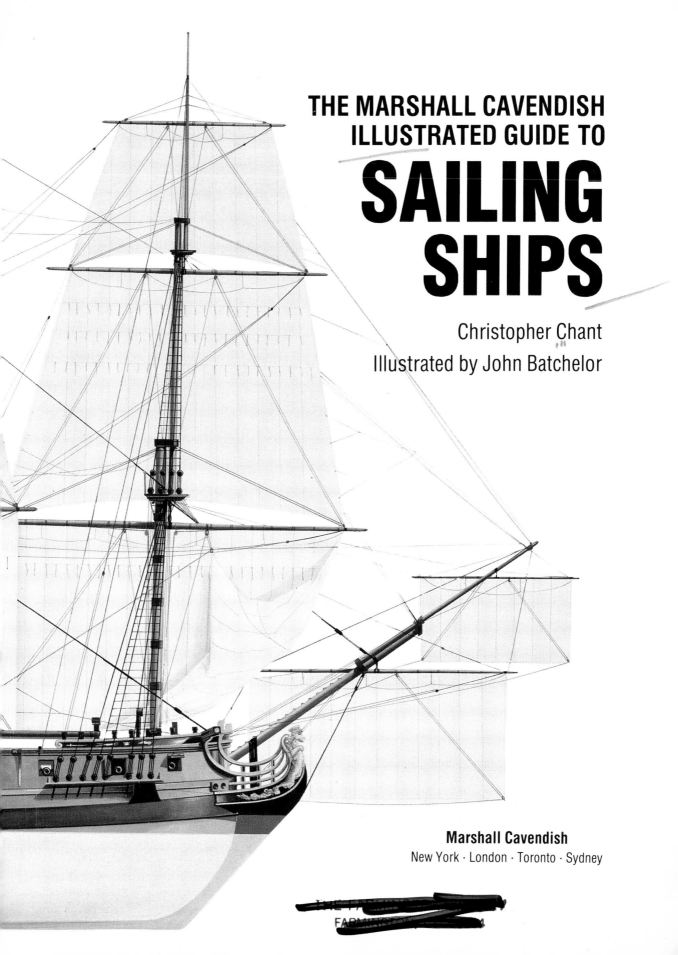

THE MARSHALL CAVENDISH ILLUSTRATED GUIDE TO
SAILING SHIPS

Christopher Chant

Illustrated by John Batchelor

Marshall Cavendish
New York · London · Toronto · Sydney

Library Edition 1989

© Marshall Cavendish Limited 1989
© DPM Services Limited 1989

Published by Marshall Cavendish Corporation
147 West Merrick Road
Freeport
Long Island
N.Y. 11520

Produced by DPM Services Limited
Designed by Graham Beehag
Illustrations © John Batchelor

Library of Congress Cataloging-in-Publication Data

Chant, Christopher.
  Sailing ships/written by Chris Chant: Illustrated by John
Batchelor.
      p.   cm – (The Marshall Cavendish illustrated guides)
  Includes index.
  Summary: Provides an illustrated history of sailing ships and
describes how they operate.
  ISBN 1-85435-091-9
  1. Sailing ships – Juvenile literature. [1. Sailing ships.]
I. Batchelor, John H., [1]. II. Title. III. Series: Chant,
Christopher. Marshall Cavendish illustrated guides.
VM531.C42 1989
387.2'043 – dc19   88-28706
                                                           CIP
                                                           AC

    ISBN 1-85435-085-4 (set).

Printed and bound in Italy by L.E.G.O. SpA, Vicenza

Sailing ships are among the most beautiful things ever made by man. In the Western world, we now know them mostly as yachts and as larger ships preserved as museums or sail training ships, but in many other parts of the world they are still working vessels. In such sailing ships, men travel lakes, rivers, shallow coastal waters, and deep oceans for trade, transport, and fishing. Indeed, it is difficult to see how most third-world countries could survive without ships and boats powered by the wind, which is free and in many parts of the world blows with great regularity. The industrial countries may no longer have to rely on the wind for power, but it is still vitally important in poorer and less industrialized countries that do not have the money and skills to import and operate the internal combustion engines we in the West take for granted.

Up to 150 years ago, when the age of steam began to produce practical and reliable coal-fired engines, the

The oldest surviving boat is a 40-ton, 142-ft. Nile boat buried near the Great Pyramid of Khufu in Egypt in about 2515 B.C. and now being reassembled as a museum exhibit.

The Viking longship could be sailed with the wind well behind the beam, but was designed mainly to be rowed. Note the steering by special oar rather than a rudder.

wind was the only alternative to muscle power for the movement of large ships and small boats. Even after the arrival of the steam engine, it was a long time before sailing ships became obsolete for everything except pleasure. The steam engine, fired by coal and then by oil, first had to prove itself in reliability and economy while driving paddle wheels and then propellers, and it was the beginning of this century before sail really gave way to steam.

For perhaps 6,000 years before that happened, sailing ships were among man's most important designs. It would be pleasant to think that we "invented" sailing, but from the beginning of time, leaves have been blown across puddles, bugs across ponds, and

branches down rivers by the power of the wind. And it is thought that the wind, working with the waves, was responsible for the migration of many plants, insects, and even animals from the mainlands to many island groups. At some unknown time in this period, a man must have seen that he could rig a primitive mast and sail (probably a pole and a fur) on a straight log to capture the wind's power and so speed his log, and he could steer his creation with his arms or a paddle. Such a primitive sailing craft would have been able to cross wide rivers and perhaps even small lakes, but would have been unable to steer very far from the way the wind was blowing.

Inventive man was soon improving this primitive

The oldest evidence for oared boats dates from the eighth millenium B.C. in the form of oars found in bogs in England and Denmark.

Ships from ancient times, such as this bireme (with two banks of oars) could again be sailed with a fair wind, but in combat were always rowed.

system. It is thought that by 4000 B.C. the Chinese were using sail-driven rafts, a model of a sailing boat used on the Tigris and Euphrates rivers has been dated by archaeologists at about 3500 B.C. and by 3400 B.C. the Egyptians were using sailing craft on rivers. Before long, the Egyptians had begun to trade along their coast and across the Mediterranean by sailing ship. Most river boats were probably made of reed bundles lashed together to make a hull with a wide and stable central section and a pointed bow and stern, which were lifted out of the water by special lashings or by a central rope connecting the bow and stern. Just in front of the central position, a short mast was placed (or stepped) with rope bracings (or stays) to the bow and stern and more bracings (or shrouds) to the sides of the hull formed by the reed bundles. These stays and shrouds held the mast upright and allowed it to carry a square sail hanging from a stout yard. The yard was controlled by rope braces running to the stern of the boat, and the bottom of the sail by further lines (sheets). Steering was entrusted to a large paddle-bladed oar lashed to hang down into the water beside or behind the stern.

Sailing ships designed for trips more than a short distance from the coast were built to the same basic pattern, but they were larger and, whenever possible,

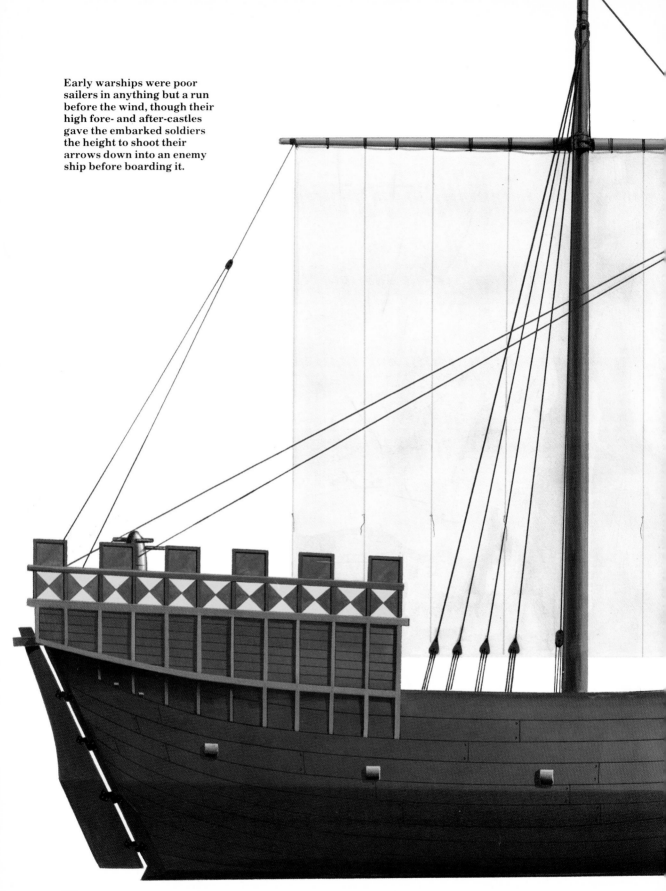

Early warships were poor sailers in anything but a run before the wind, though their high fore- and after-castles gave the embarked soldiers the height to shoot their arrows down into an enemy ship before boarding it.

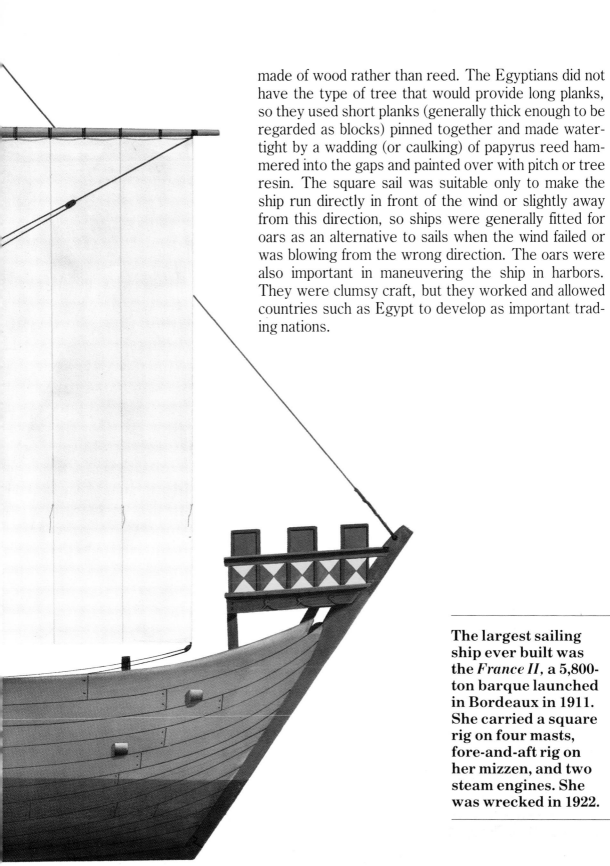

made of wood rather than reed. The Egyptians did not have the type of tree that would provide long planks, so they used short planks (generally thick enough to be regarded as blocks) pinned together and made watertight by a wadding (or caulking) of papyrus reed hammered into the gaps and painted over with pitch or tree resin. The square sail was suitable only to make the ship run directly in front of the wind or slightly away from this direction, so ships were generally fitted for oars as an alternative to sails when the wind failed or was blowing from the wrong direction. The oars were also important in maneuvering the ship in harbors. They were clumsy craft, but they worked and allowed countries such as Egypt to develop as important trading nations.

The largest sailing ship ever built was the *France II*, a 5,800-ton barque launched in Bordeaux in 1911. She carried a square rig on four masts, fore-and-aft rig on her mizzen, and two steam engines. She was wrecked in 1922.

The Western sailing
vessel with the most
masts was the seven-
masted schooner
Thomas W. Lawson, a
5,218-ton vessel
launched in
Massachusetts in
1905 and lost in the
English channel in
1907.

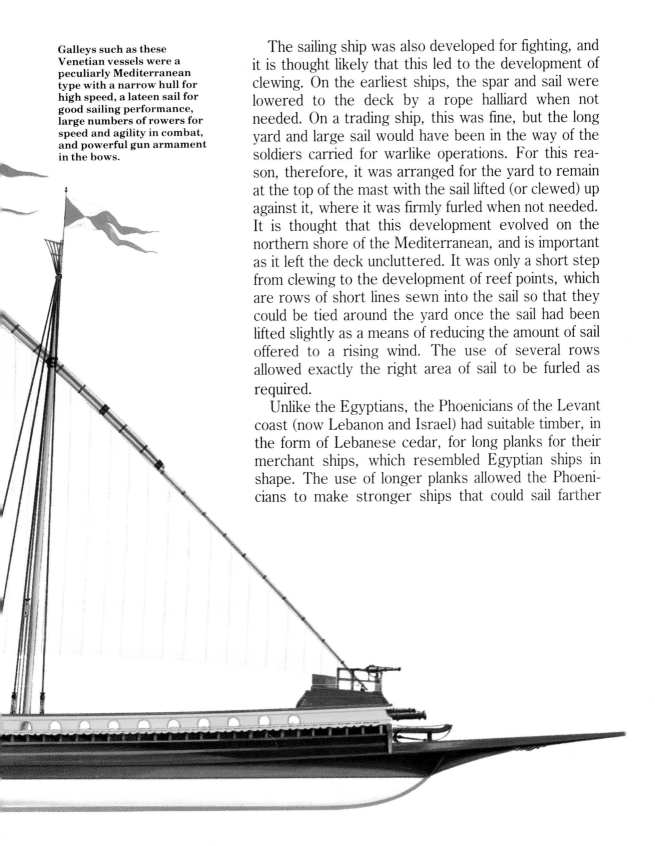

The sailing ship was also developed for fighting, and it is thought likely that this led to the development of clewing. On the earliest ships, the spar and sail were lowered to the deck by a rope halliard when not needed. On a trading ship, this was fine, but the long yard and large sail would have been in the way of the soldiers carried for warlike operations. For this reason, therefore, it was arranged for the yard to remain at the top of the mast with the sail lifted (or clewed) up against it, where it was firmly furled when not needed. It is thought that this development evolved on the northern shore of the Mediterranean, and is important as it left the deck uncluttered. It was only a short step from clewing to the development of reef points, which are rows of short lines sewn into the sail so that they could be tied around the yard once the sail had been lifted slightly as a means of reducing the amount of sail offered to a rising wind. The use of several rows allowed exactly the right area of sail to be furled as required.

Unlike the Egyptians, the Phoenicians of the Levant coast (now Lebanon and Israel) had suitable timber, in the form of Lebanese cedar, for long planks for their merchant ships, which resembled Egyptian ships in shape. The use of longer planks allowed the Phoenicians to make stronger ships that could sail farther

from the coast and brave worse weather. Therefore, they could undertake longer voyages, which included, it is thought, a three-year expedition around Africa in the 7th century B.C. The Phoenicians were also the first to develop a ship especially for war. It was a narrow type that could be sailed before any favorable wind, but which was fitted with one, two, or even three banks of oars for speed and maneuverability in naval battles. Despite these important developments, the Phoenicians lacked the engineering skill to make ships that were notably larger than those of the Egyptians. It was the Greeks, and to a larger extent, the Romans who built the Western world's first large ships after developing the idea of a large and very strong frame on which was laid an arrangement of caulked planks to provide a watertight hull.

The leader of the first expedition to circumnavigate the globe was Fernai de Magalhaes, a Portuguese better known as Ferdinand Magellan. The expedition of five Spanish-sponsored ships departed Spain in September, 1519, and after crossing the Atlantic passed around Cape Horn and across the Pacific to the Philippines, where Magellan was killed. One ship finally reached Seville in July, 1522, with only 31 of the 270 men who had set out on the expedition.

The Romans were responsible for the creation of what can be called the modern sailing ship. The Roman structure was based on a strong keel running from bow to stern, where uprights called the stem and sternpost rose to give the ship strength against the buffeting of the waves. The shape of the hull was given by large frames rising from the keel and held in place by the stringers that ran in wide curves from the stem to the sternpost. Over this frame was laid the hull planking and the deck sections to create a large, hollow interior.

Two masts allowed more sail area to be carried, thus giving better outright performance, and also offered a more balanced arrangement of sail so that the vessel handled better.

The system allowed the building of larger, as well as more seaworthy ships, and this in turn opened the way for tub-like merchantmen and sword-like fighting ships. The one or two-masted merchantmen were wide and slow, but were well suited to the task of carrying the bulk of Rome's enormous trade. The warships were fast and maneuverable, and the use of clewed sails allowed them to sail rapidly into battle and get the sails out of the way quickly so that the banks of oarsmen could get to work. Enemy ships were rammed with the warship's long reinforced bow and left to sink, or boarded and captured by soldiers who were carried for just this purpose.

The Roman shipbuilders used planks laid side by side (carvel construction) to produce a smooth finish next to the water. This basic structure and finish was standard across Europe until the decline of the Roman empire in the 5th century A.D. It remained the most widely used method of shipbuilding in the Mediterranean after this time, but as Roman influence in northern Europe waned, the Roman techniques were largely lost.

The earliest known indication of sailing vessels is a clay model, apparently of such a craft and dated to about 3,500 B.C., discovered at Eridu in the plain of the Tigris and Euphrates rivers of modern Iraq.

Three-masted lateen rig on a large hull with a rudder.

17

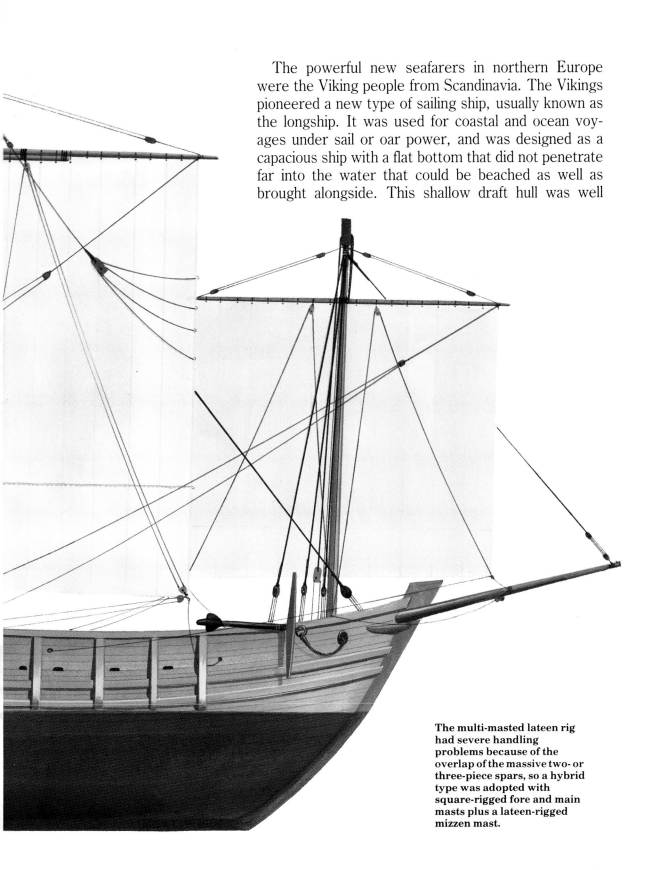

The powerful new seafarers in northern Europe were the Viking people from Scandinavia. The Vikings pioneered a new type of sailing ship, usually known as the longship. It was used for coastal and ocean voyages under sail or oar power, and was designed as a capacious ship with a flat bottom that did not penetrate far into the water that could be beached as well as brought alongside. This shallow draft hull was well

The multi-masted lateen rig had severe handling problems because of the overlap of the massive two- or three-piece spars, so a hybrid type was adopted with square-rigged fore and main masts plus a lateen-rigged mizzen mast.

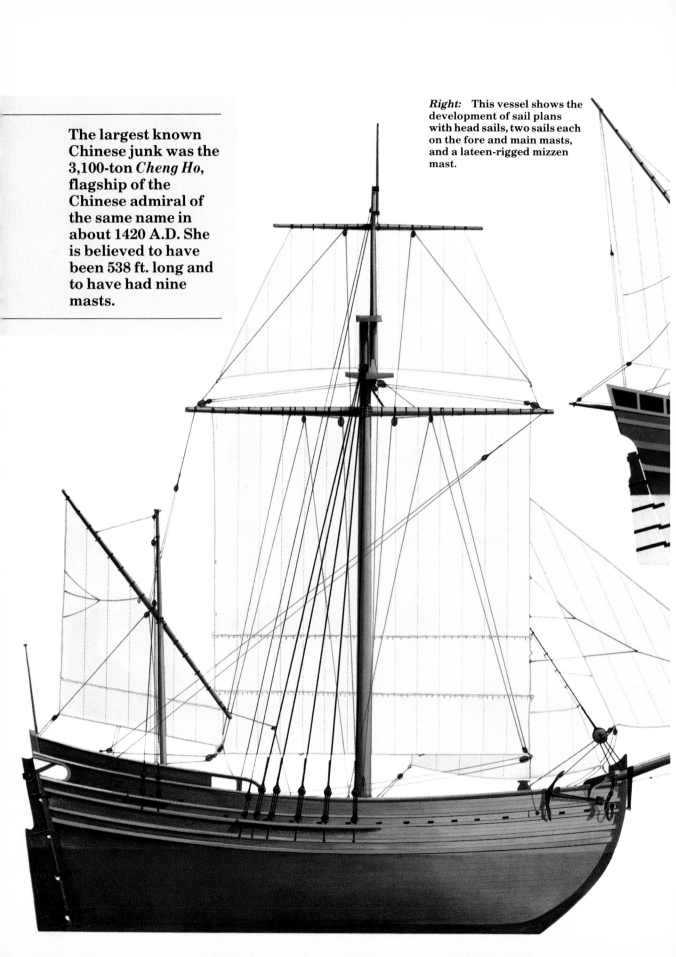

The largest known Chinese junk was the 3,100-ton *Cheng Ho*, flagship of the Chinese admiral of the same name in about 1420 A.D. She is believed to have been 538 ft. long and to have had nine masts.

Right: This vessel shows the development of sail plans with head sails, two sails each on the fore and main masts, and a lateen-rigged mizzen mast.

The adoption of the bowsprit allowed a number of fore-and-aft head sails to be set, with advantages in sailing to windward and in tacking.

suited to conditions in northern Europe: the Vikings could beach their ships for safety in the winter, and in the summer, they used them to push deep into fjords and rivers on their raiding and trading voyages. The Viking ships were like those of the Phoenicians in being long and thin, but like those of the Romans in being built up on a frame. Northern Europe had lost the technique of carvel planking, and the longships were clinker-built, with the lower edge of each plank overlapping the upper edge of the plank below it.

Driven before the wind by a single square sail or moved by its oars, the longship was ideally suited to the Vikings' way of life. The Vikings also discovered that the yard could be braced far around, so that the sail was angled more to the hull than running across it, and this allowed the longship to sail crabwise into the general direction of the wind in a zigzag maneuver known as tacking. In their longships, these adventurous people traded through the rivers of eastern Europe to reach the Black Sea, sailed around the coasts of western Europe to enter the Mediterranean through the Straits of Gibraltar, and most impressively of all, sailed west into the Atlantic to discover and settle Iceland, Greenland, and even North America before 1000 A.D.

The caravela rotunda had a plain bow, square-rigged fore and main masts, and a lateen-rigged mizzen mast.

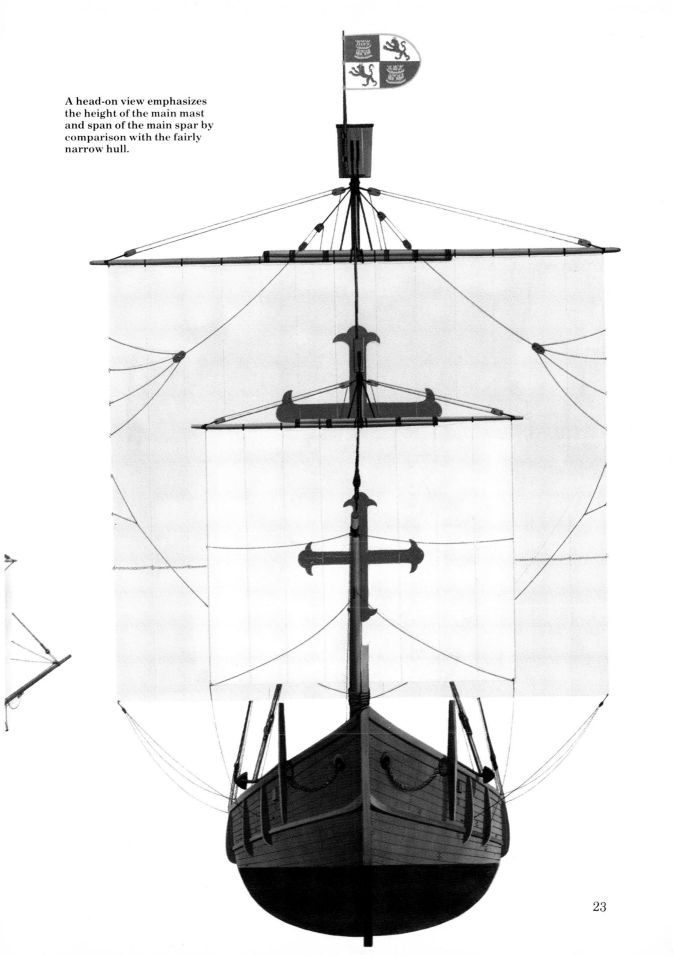

A head-on view emphasizes
the height of the main mast
and span of the main spar by
comparison with the fairly
narrow hull.

As the northern Europeans began to come out of the Dark Ages that followed the fall of Rome, its seafaring peoples began to build up an important trade network using a small but stout ship that combined the layout of the Mediterranean ship (a fat hull and two or sometimes three masts) with the Viking type of clinker construction. The trade network grew rapidly up to about 1000 A.D. and during this period, oars generally disappeared from northern European ships. Merchants were trying to save money by reducing the size of crews, while improved layout and skills meant that ships could more easily use the Viking-discovered ability of ships to sail into the general direction of the wind by bracing the yards around. Speed for its own sake was not important to traders, whose ships were therefore wide for their length to increase their cargo-

Left: **A 17th century Portuguese carrack of the type evolved from the caravela rotunda with greater size and beam, fore- and after-castles, and an improvement in overall seaworthiness.**

Below: **An early example of the carrack type of vessel.**

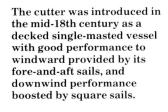

The cutter was introduced in the mid-18th century as a decked single-masted vessel with good performance to windward provided by its fore-and-aft sails, and downwind performance boosted by square sails.

carrying capacity amd make them simple to sail with small crews.

At much the same time, larger carvel-built merchant ships with two or three masts began to appear. Each one carried a single square sail on each of the masts, but as ships increased in size, the masts were lengthened by adding one or two more sections above the main mast, each section carrying its own sail in an arrangement that allowed exactly the right adjustment of sails for all weathers and conditions. Ships were becoming more maneuverable, and in the 12th century the sharply sloped stern began to disappear in favor of a more upright kind that could take a hinged rudder. With this development, the steering oar disappeared, and ships became not only easier, but also more precise to handle. The true rudder and square sails could be braced far around toward the side of the ship.

Together, they provided the ability to sail in any direction except directly into or close to the wind, and it was possible to make headway in these directions by tacking. This improvement marked the end of oared ships in northern Europe, where rough weather is common: but in the Mediterranean, oared warships remained in service until after the beginning of the 18th century.

The main types of trading ship employed in the Mediterranean in the period from the 14th to the 17th

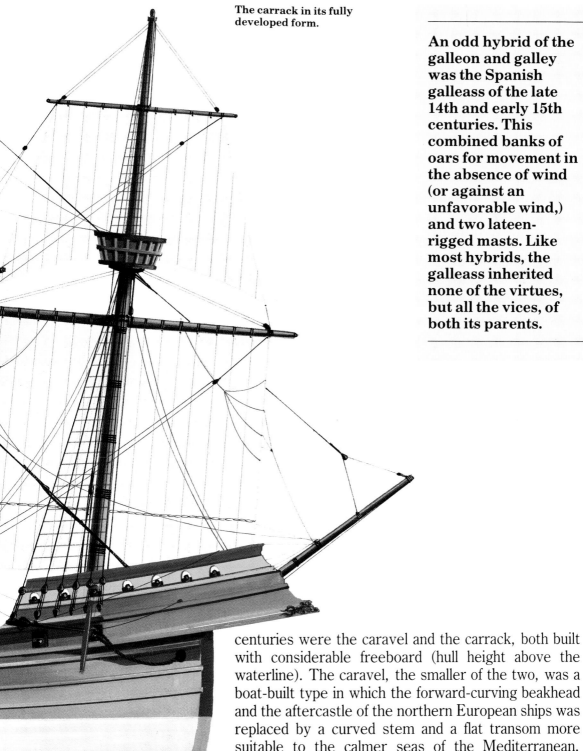

The carrack in its fully developed form.

An odd hybrid of the galleon and galley was the Spanish galleass of the late 14th and early 15th centuries. This combined banks of oars for movement in the absence of wind (or against an unfavorable wind,) and two lateen-rigged masts. Like most hybrids, the galleass inherited none of the virtues, but all the vices, of both its parents.

centuries were the caravel and the carrack, both built with considerable freeboard (hull height above the waterline). The caravel, the smaller of the two, was a boat-built type in which the forward-curving beakhead and the aftercastle of the northern European ships was replaced by a curved stem and a flat transom more suitable to the calmer seas of the Mediterranean. These vessels were generally two-masted, with a single lateen (triangular fore-and-aft) sail on each mast, and were able to sail closer to the wind than the square-rigged north European vessels. The Spanish and Portuguese began to use the caravel in the 16th century and soon found that the lateen rig was not suitable for long ocean voyages. These two great exploring nations therefore developed the caravel into a three-masted type with square sails on the two forward masts and a lateen-rigged mizzen mast. The three ships of Christopher Columbus' voyage across the Atlantic in 1492 were caravels. The Santa Maria

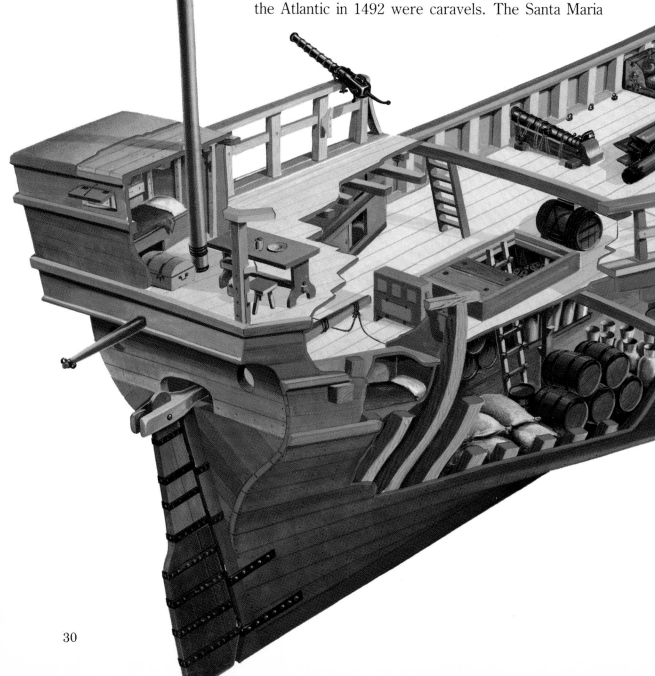

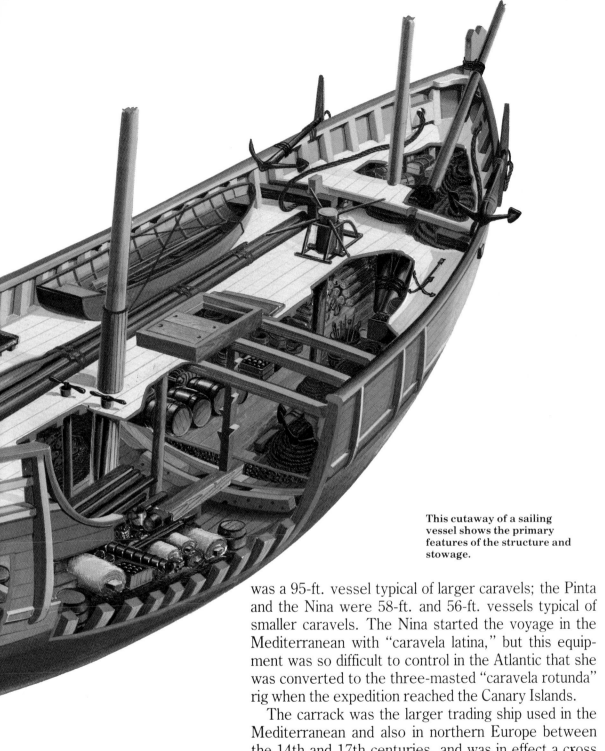

This cutaway of a sailing vessel shows the primary features of the structure and stowage.

was a 95-ft. vessel typical of larger caravels; the Pinta and the Nina were 58-ft. and 56-ft. vessels typical of smaller caravels. The Nina started the voyage in the Mediterranean with "caravela latina," but this equipment was so difficult to control in the Atlantic that she was converted to the three-masted "caravela rotunda" rig when the expedition reached the Canary Islands.

The carrack was the larger trading ship used in the Mediterranean and also in northern Europe between the 14th and 17th centuries, and was in effect a cross between the lateen-rigged Mediterranean ship and the square-rigged north European ship. It was thus similar to the fully developed caravel with three masts, but was larger and broader in the beam with a displacement of up to 1,200 tons. The carrack was generally of

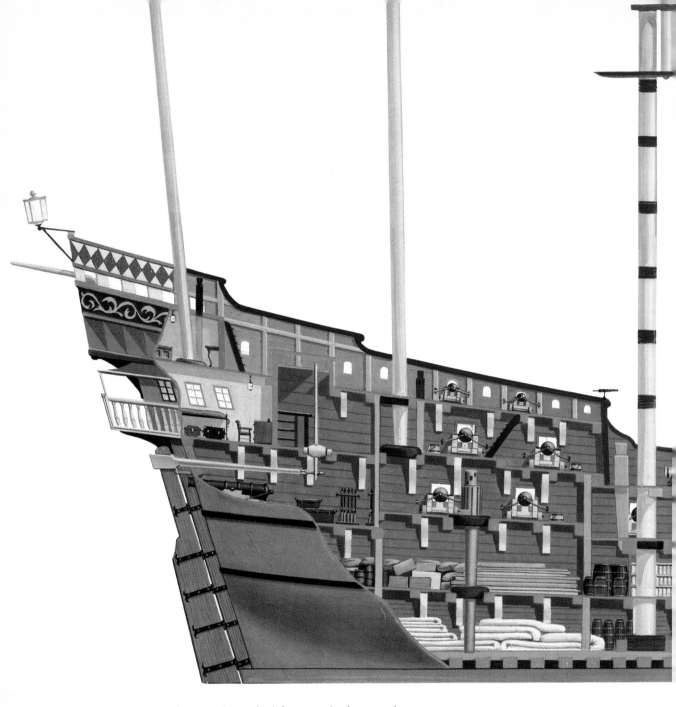

sturdy construction, and carried fore-and aftercastles. The carrack was the first example of the "typical" trading ship that lasted until the arrival of steam, with square-rigged fore and main masts, plus a lateen-rigged mizzen mast. The only real development in the carrack resulted in the galleon. This design eliminated the high forecastle with its tendency to blow the bow down wind, resulting in a ship that was able to sail closer to the wind.

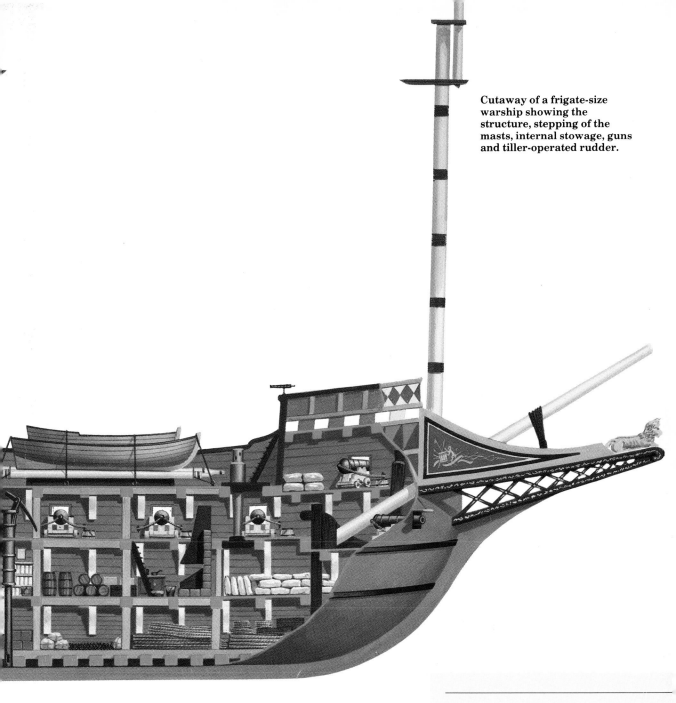

Except for the lateen on the mizzen, ships were rigged with square sails until the middle of the 17th century. By this time, the lateen had begun to give way to the more manageable spritsail, which was rigged completely aft of the mast with a diagonal spar running from low on the mast to the rear upper corner of the spritsail. The evolution was completed when the spritsail was replaced by the four-sided spanker, or driver, with a boom at its foot and a gaff at its head.

The largest number of competitors ever to start in a sailboat race was 1,261 in a 233-mile race around the island of Zealand in Denmark during June, 1976.

The driver was initially considered a fair-weather sail, but its easy tacking meant that it finally replaced the lowest square sail on the mizzen (the mizzen course) after the middle of the 18th century.

Square-rigged ships work best when running before the wind, whereas ships with fore-and-aft rigs can sail closer to the wind. By the middle of the 17th century, serious efforts were being made to combine the two

Right: The fully-rigged sail training ship *Gorch Fock* under sail.

Below: The barque-rigged *Pamir* under way.

types of rig to produce a sailing ship able to run before or tack into the wind with equal ease. The mizzen spritsail was a move in the right direction, but greater capability came from the adoption of staysails and jibs. Staysails are triangular sails set on the stays that brace the masts against fore-and-aft movement, while the jibs, also triangular, are set on the stays bracing the foremast to the bowsprit, running forward from the bow and previously used for a spritsail (below) and a small square sail (above).

As trade increased in volume and importance during the 19th century, greater emphasis was placed on speed, as well as on smaller crews for higher profits. The handling of fore-and-aft rigs requires fewer men than square rigs, and ship designers combined the two basic types of rig in the ships of the period. The larger ships were the barque and barquentine. The barque

displaced up to 5,500 tons and had between three and five masts, of which the forward two were always square-rigged. The barquentine had three masts and was square-rigged only on the foremast. The smaller ships were the brig and brigantine. The brig is a two-masted ship square-rigged on both masts, while the brigantine is also two-masted, but square-rigged on only the foremast.

The ultimate in sailing vessels able to sail to windward is the schooner, which began to appear at the beginning of the 18th century in Massachusetts as a fairly small, two-or three-masted vessel fore-and-aft rigged on all its masts. They were fast and extremely weatherly vessels, at first carrying four-sided main sails, but from the middle of the 18th century, increasingly seen with the Bermudan rig, which replaces four-sided sails with triangular sails that have their heads at the top of the

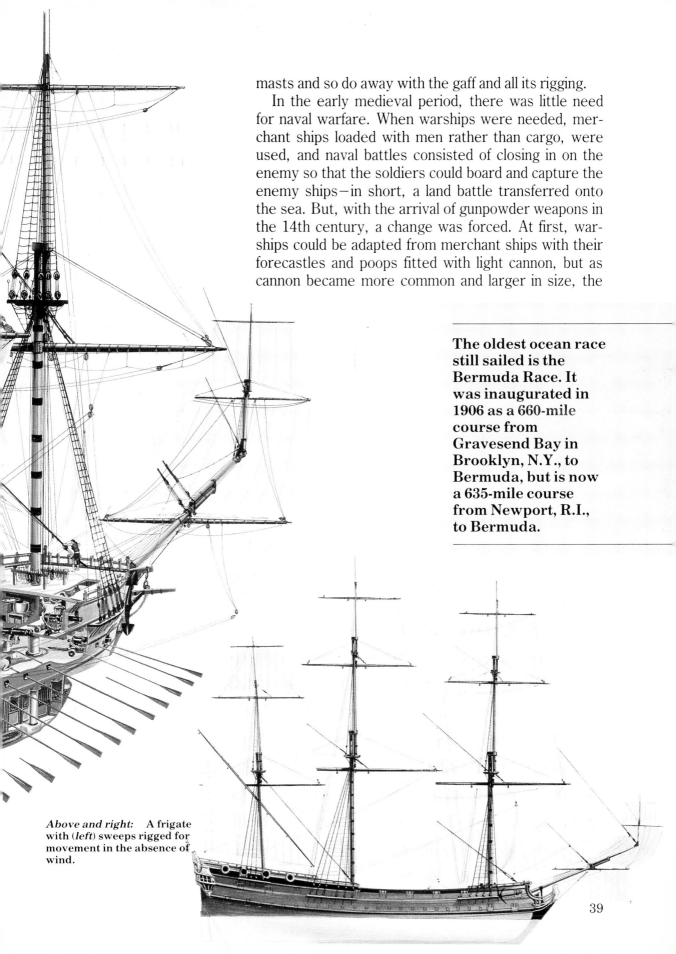

masts and so do away with the gaff and all its rigging.

In the early medieval period, there was little need for naval warfare. When warships were needed, merchant ships loaded with men rather than cargo, were used, and naval battles consisted of closing in on the enemy so that the soldiers could board and capture the enemy ships — in short, a land battle transferred onto the sea. But, with the arrival of gunpowder weapons in the 14th century, a change was forced. At first, warships could be adapted from merchant ships with their forecastles and poops fitted with light cannon, but as cannon became more common and larger in size, the

The oldest ocean race still sailed is the Bermuda Race. It was inaugurated in 1906 as a 660-mile course from Gravesend Bay in Brooklyn, N.Y., to Bermuda, but is now a 635-mile course from Newport, R.I., to Bermuda.

Above and right: A frigate with (*left*) sweeps rigged for movement in the absence of wind.

39

ships became too top heavy. So, warships became longer and lower, with the cannon arranged in broadside rows along the length of the upper deck. At the same time, the forecastles and poops were made taller so that light weapons could be mounted in and on them to attack the enemy ship's crew and, in the event that the ship was boarded, to shoot down into the enemy fighting in the waist of the ship between the forward and aft "castles." The scheme worked well when the ships were actually fighting, but it made them difficult to sail, as the large area of the forecastle and poop allowed the wind to push the ship sideways.

These early warships were of about 500 tons, though some English warships were as large as 1,000 tons. Late in the 16th century, English shipbuilders began to develop warships with lower "castles," especially at the bow. These ships were so much better at sailing that they could outmaneuver their enemies and use their guns in positions from which the enemy could not reply. Larger numbers of guns were installed by increasing the height of the hull and arranging the guns on separate decks. This English development was soon copied by other European navies to produce hard-hitting ships that could also sail well.

This established the pattern of warships until well into the 19th century. Refinements were made, but the basic pattern remained unaltered, despite a growth

A later frigate cut away to reveal internal features such as the mechanical (though man-powered) pump for the removal of water from the bilges.

in size to about 3,000 tons and 130 guns by the middle of the 19th century. The emphasis in warship design was on speed and agility, calling for a long, comparatively narrow hull, which improved the warship's ability to carry the long rows of guns needed to fire effective broadside salvos. By the middle of the 18th century, the increasing formality of naval warfare had led most navies to introduce special designations for their warships. Ships were designated by the number of their guns into six "rates." The first three, and sometimes the fourth, were "line of battle ships," while the fifth and sixth were frigates designed to scout for the heavier vessels. The exact number of guns that decided the rate varied slightly with date, but at the time of Lord Nelson's Battle of Trafalgar in 1805, a first rate had more than 100 guns, a second rate between 84 and 100, a third rate between 70 and 84, a fourth rate between 50 and 70, a fifth rate between 32 and 50, and a sixth rate below 32. The need of the larger ships to accommodate the guns on up to three gun decks led to the development of warships that were comparatively tall. To reduce stability problems, the hulls were given great "tumblehome," the attractive inward curve of the hull above the point of greatest beam.

The heaviest guns were placed as low as possible to reduce stability problems still further, and the guns were fired through port holes in the hull that were

The fastest crossing of the Atlantic under sail was achieved in June, 1988, by the French single-handed sailor Philippe Poupon in the British-designed trimaran *Michel Fleuron*. He covered the 2,800 miles from Plymouth, UK, to Newport, Rhode Island, in 10 days, 9 hours, 15 minutes, and 9 seconds at an average speed of about 13 knots.

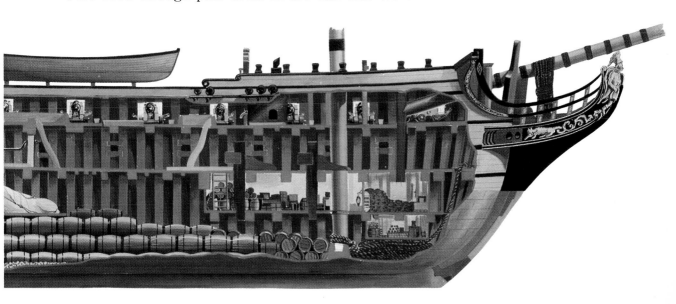

The warship of the time of the Napoleonic Wars was a highly developed and intricate piece of sailing machinery capable of exceptional sailing performance when handled with skill.

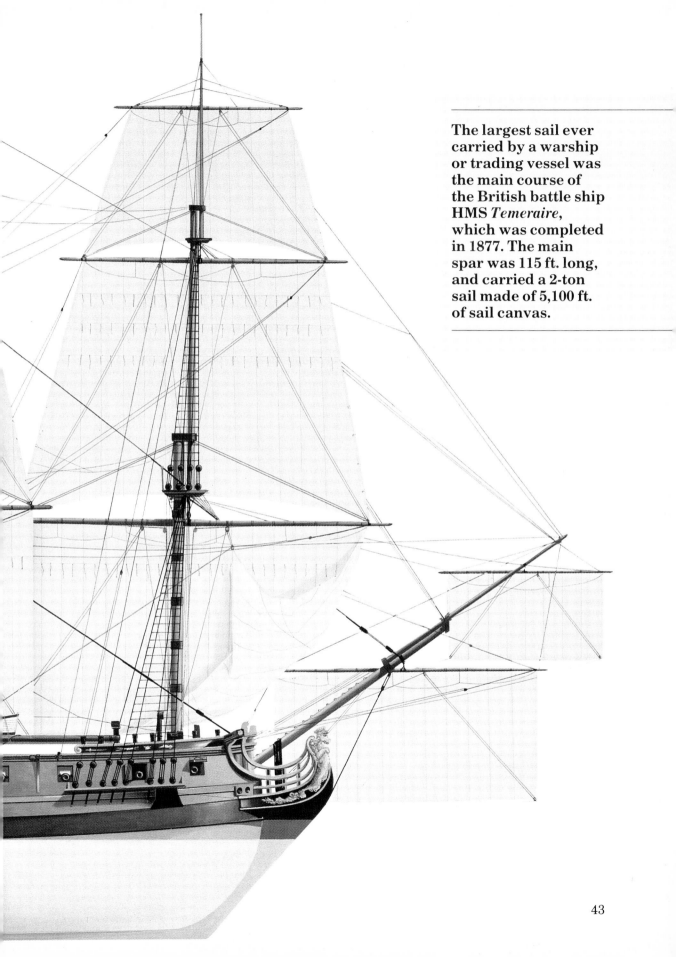

The largest sail ever
carried by a warship
or trading vessel was
the main course of
the British battle ship
HMS *Temeraire*,
which was completed
in 1877. The main
spar was 115 ft. long,
and carried a 2-ton
sail made of 5,100 ft.
of sail canvas.

covered by heavy port lids when the guns were not being used. The guns had long barrels and were extremely heavy, recoiling far inboard when fired and requiring heavy tackles to stop them from sliding. The recoil brought the muzzle inboard of the port lid, which allowed these muzzle-loading weapons to be reloaded without undue difficulty before being run out again to their firing positions. The effective range of naval cannon was only about 100 yards, so naval battles were generally side-by-side slugging matches in which weight of fire (the weight of the ball fired and the number of rounds fired) counted more than pinpoint accuracy; the largest cannon carried by first-rate ships fired a 42-lb. ball, and the lightest standard cannon fired an 18-lb. ball. The tendency toward weight of fire reached its height in the Napoleonic wars, when the carronade was introduced as a short-range "smasher." To reduce its recoil, this ship's gun was mounted on a slide rather than wheels, and was a notably inaccurate weapon designed to fire a large ball over a short range. Solid shot was designed to penetrate thick hull planking, and other projectiles were used to knock down masts, rigging, and men.

The warships led the way in the development of sailing techniques during the 15th, 16th, and 17th centuries. To move bulk cargoes at the lowest cost, merchant traders were still in favor of large hulls moved by two square sails on each of three masts, typical of the 250-ton caravel that was the most important trading ship until the end of the 14th century. But the opening of new transoceanic trade routes to the east and west as a result of the "Age of Discovery" opened the way for larger and more weatherly ships, such as the Spanish high-forecastle carracks and their successors, the low-forecastle galleons of up to 1,600 tons. The merchant companies formed by most northern European countries to conduct the trade to India and the Far East, used another successor of the carrack, the East Indiamen. The development of this luxury trade began to place increasing emphasis on fast delivery, and these ships became larger than warships, with fine hull lines for speed combined with carrying capacity. Tall masts with huge clouds of sail became

The greatest seaborne expedition of the era of sail was the Spanish Armada launched against England in 1588 under the Duke of Medina Sidonia. The fleet comprised 130 ships that left Lisbon in May, 1588, and after passing into the English Channel to collect the army of the Duke of Parma from Flanders, was harried by the English and the weather. Eventually driven into the North Sea by the weather, the Armada made for home around the north of Scotland and west of Ireland, suffering severe losses and returning to Spain with only 67 ships.

Left: **The beak head, bowsprit and masts of one of history's most celebrated sailships, HMS *Victory* that was Admiral Lord Nelson's flagship at the Battle of Trafalgar in 1805.**

As it had need for fewer men and only a light armament, the merchant ship was devoted to great freight stowage, a factor aided by the design that emphasized internal volume rather than the fine lines needed for good performance in all but the clipper ships.

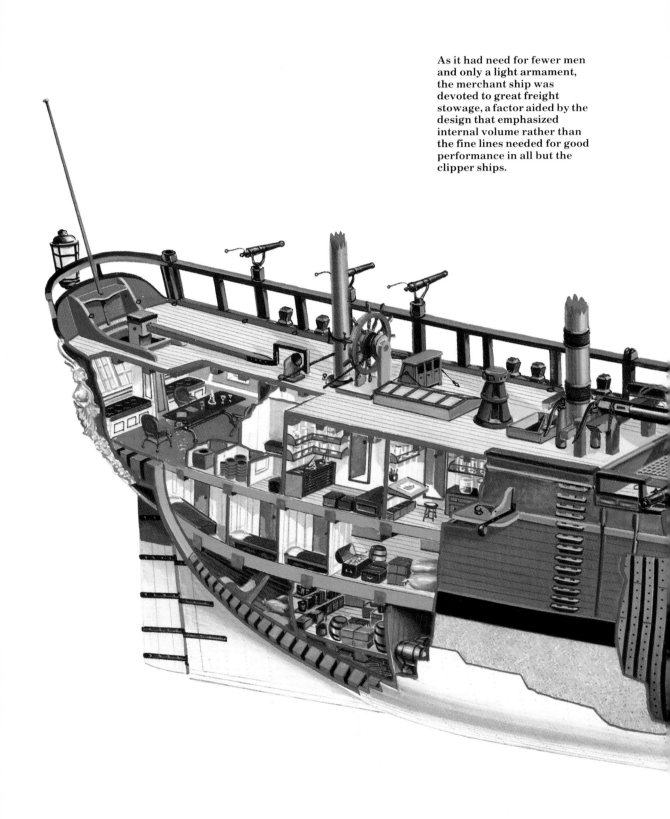

common, and larger crews allowed these superb sailing vessels to be sailed to their limits over massive distances. The wool trade with Australia and the tea trade with China were dominated by the great clipper ships until the opening of the Suez Canal in 1869, when the steamship began to rival the clipper on long routes to the eastern hemisphere. The last place where the great sailing ships still held an edge was South America, where European and American traders needed to round Cape Horn. The sailing ships made the perilous journey more easily than the early steamships, and

The longest single-day run ever claimed by a sailing vessel is 535 miles by the 2,722-ton clipper *Champion of the Seas* on December 11/12, 1854, running before a northwest gale in the southern part of the Indian Ocean. It is highly unlikely that this distance was actually achieved.

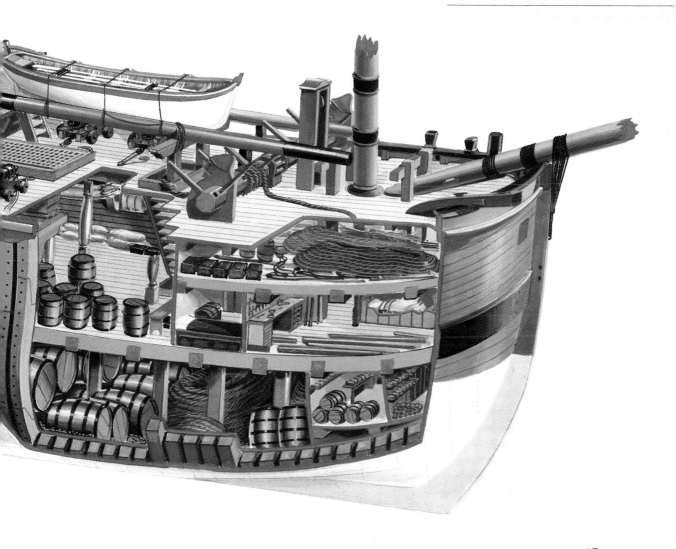

Right: A whaling boat complete with oars, a mast and sails, harpoons and a great length of line connecting the harpoon to the boat.

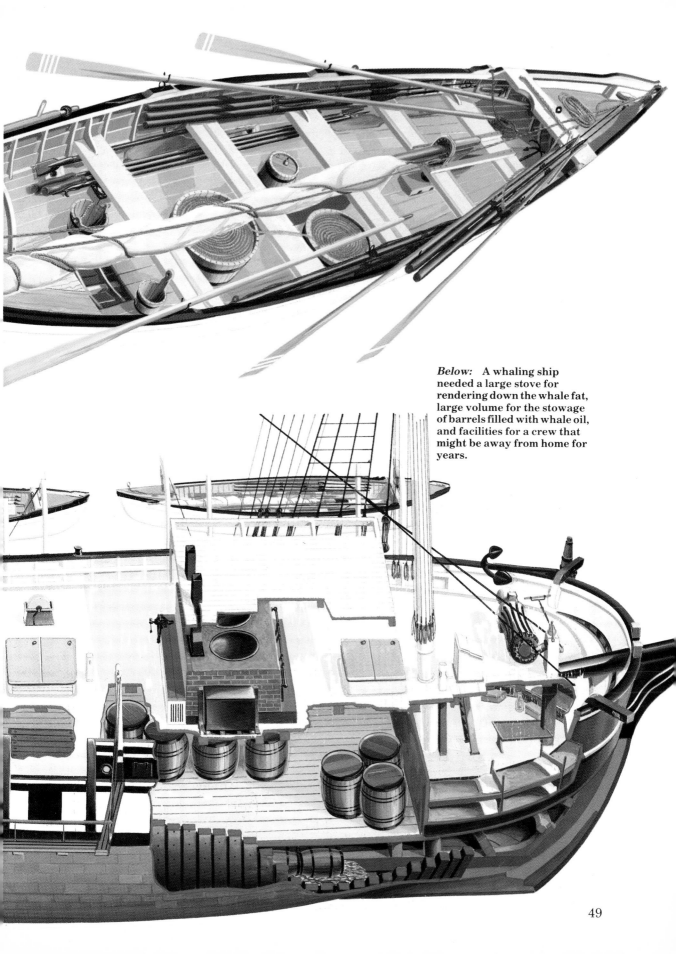

Below: A whaling ship needed a large stove for rendering down the whale fat, large volume for the stowage of barrels filled with whale oil, and facilities for a crew that might be away from home for years.

49

The old and the new: a Bell
Model 206 JetRanger
helicopter passes the
American sail training ship
Eagle, a German ship taken
over by the Americans at the
end of World War II.

The America's Cup
race series is so
named for the
unnamed silver cup
won in 1851 by the US
schooner *America* in a
race around the Isle
of Wight off the south
coast of England.
The cup was later
given to the New
York Yacht Club as a
challenge trophy,
and was not lost by
the club until it was
taken by an
Australian 12-meter
yacht in 1982.

The world's longest yacht race is the four-yearly Whitbread Round the World Race, first sailed in 1973. It covers a round-trip course of 30,150 miles to and from Portsmouth, UK, after stops in Cape Town, South Africa; Auckland, New Zealand; and Rio de Janeiro, Brazil.

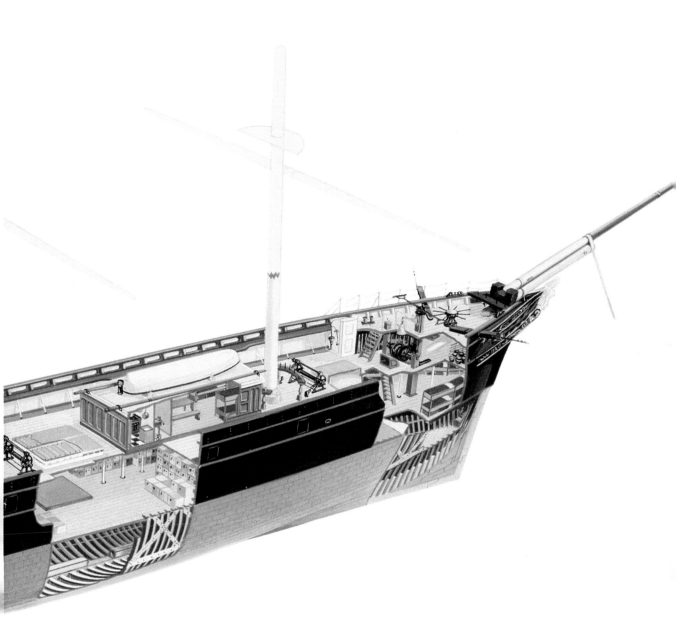

large four-masted barques and five-masted schooners were the best ships on this route until 1914. In that year, the Panama Canal was opened, and this passage between the Caribbean and the Pacific Ocean removed most of the need for ships to sail around Cape Horn.

World War I ended the day of the sailing ship as the chief trading vessel of the advanced countries: German submarine and surface raiders sank many sailing ships that lacked the speed to escape, and the Allies concentrated their shipbuilding on the steam-driven ships that

Details of the innards and the construction of a merchant sailing ship in the great days of the 19th century.

Right: A head-on view highlights the enormous width of a clipper ship with all her stunning sails (pronounced stunsails) set. These were used only in fair weather with the wind well abaft the beam.

Left: In areas not well served by roads or railroads, the sailboat has been a useful transport until modern times. These are firewood carriers in northern Portugal.

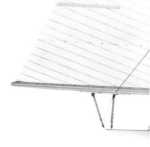

were already in a dominant position. By the middle of the 1970s, the large sailing ship had disappeared, with the exception of some 35 ships used for sail training. Larger numbers of smaller sailing vessels survive as leisure and training vessels in the more advanced countries, and vast numbers of small sail-powered vessels survive in the Far East and Pacific. In the Far East, they serve a vital function on the rivers of China and in the coastal and inter-island waters of southeast Asia and the 13,000 Indonesian islands. In the Pacific, sail-

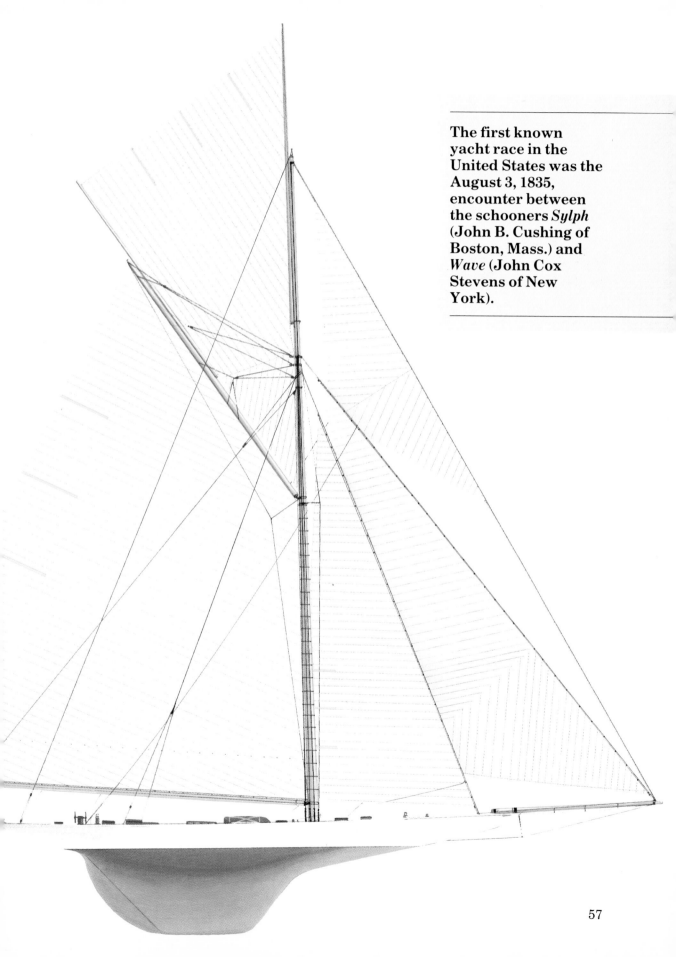

The first known
yacht race in the
United States was the
August 3, 1835,
encounter between
the schooners *Sylph*
(John B. Cushing of
Boston, Mass.) and
Wave (John Cox
Stevens of New
York).

Left: The 12-meter yachts
Freedom (US-30) and
Australia battle it out in the
1982 America's Cup series
that finally lost the New York
Yacht Club this celebrated
trophy for the first time in its
history.

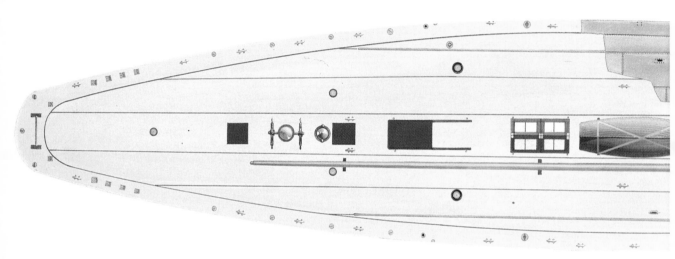

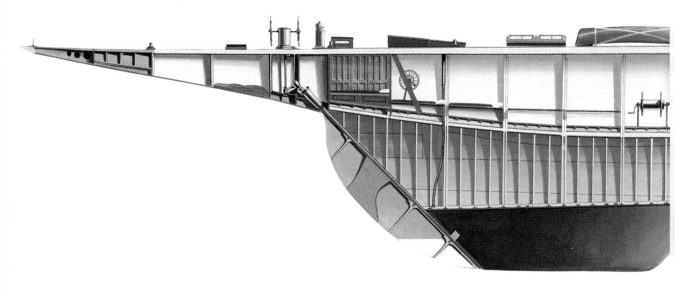

ing vessels are still the most important trade and communication link in that vast ocean's island groups.

In the Western world, the most important use of sail today is for recreation and competitive sport, ranging from small dinghies with centerboards instead of keels, through twin-hulled catamarans and three-hulled trimarans used for long-distance cruising and oceanic races, to the "blue ribbon" offshore racing boats with a length of 75 ft. and a substantial crew. Undoubtedly, the best known of the racing sailboats are the 12-meter yachts used in the America's Cup series up to 1988. Yachting

The most successful yacht in history was _Britannia_, owned by King Edward VII and then by King George V. In a career from 1893 to 1935, she raced 625 times and won 231 times.

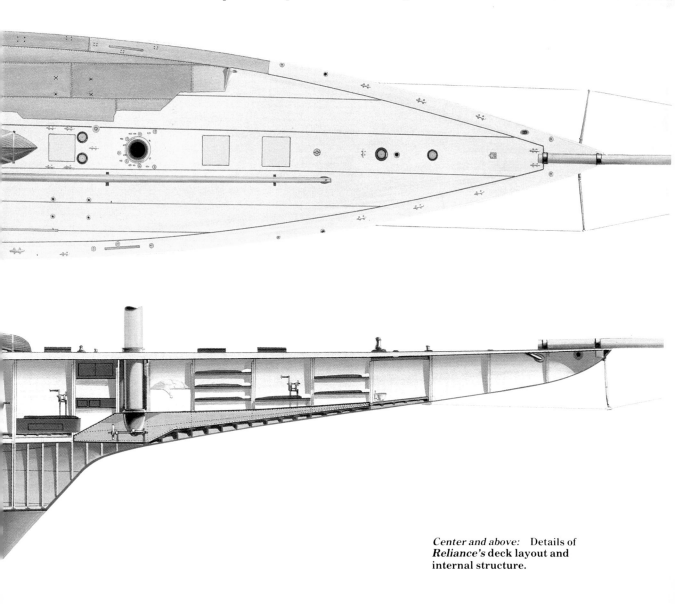

Center and above: Details of *Reliance's* deck layout and internal structure.

has been popular with the rich since the middle of the 17th century and became increasingly widespread in the 18th and 19th centuries. But it is only in the 20th century that sailboats have become as immensely popular as they are today, catering for every degree of skill, enthusiasm, and wealth.

Below: The converted 12-meter yacht *American Eagle* leads another American boat, the maxi-yacht *Kialoa II,* during a 1971 Southern Cross Cup race.

The longest established yacht race in European waters is the Fastnet Race, which was inaugurated in 1925 as a race from Ryde on the Isle of Wight around the Fastnet Rock off the southwest coast of Ireland to a finish off Plymouth in Devon.

Typical of modern cruiser racers is the Moody "Sigma 33" type, offering a good blend of cruising comfort and racing performance.

Glossary

Aftercastle: fighting platform raised above the stern of the ship, evolved from the poop
Barque: three- to five-masted vessel in which the forward two masts are square-rigged
Barquentine: three-masted vessel in which the forward two are square-rigged
Boom: spar attached to the foot of a sail, and generally attached at its forward end to the mast
Bow: front of a boat or ship
Bowsprit: an upward-angled "mast" projecting forward from the bow to carry the foremast's forestays
Brace: rope used to control the backward and forward swinging movement of a spar
Brig: two-masted vessel square-rigged on both masts
Brigantine: two-masted vessel square-rigged only on the foremast
Caraval: ship with bow and flat transom
Carrack: development of the caravel with larger size, fore- and aftercastles, and a beaked bow
Carvel construction: type of hull construction with the longitudinal planks laid edge to edge
Catamaran: boat in which two equal hulls are connected above the waterline
Caulking: matter pushed into the joints between planks to make them watertight
Clinker construction: type of hull construction with the lengthwise planks laid so that the bottom of one overlaps the top of the next plank down
Course: the lowest and largest square-rigged sail attached to any mast
Draft: the depth of the hull between the waterline and the bottom of the keel
Forecastle: raised structure at the bow of a ship, originally developed for warships
Frame: structural member rising from the keel to give the hull its shape when covered with longitudinal planking
Furling: bunching a sail against its spar and lashing it firmly out of the way
Gaff: equivalent to the spar at the head of a four-sided sail, and generally attached at its forward end to the mast
Galleon: development of the carrack without the high forecastle
Halliard: rope used to hoist a spar or sail to the masthead
Hull: body of a boat or ship
Jib: triangular sail attached to any of the stays connecting the foremast with the bow or bowsprit
Keel: main structural member running the length of the lower hull from stempost to sternpost

Lateen sail: triangular fore-and-aft sail hanging from a spar

Mast: upright pole rising from the hull to support the sail(s)

Mizzenmast: the aftermost of several masts

Poop: raised section at the stern of a ship

Raft: flat floating platform of logs, planks etc., tied together

Reefing: reducing the area of sail by lifting its bottom edge and tying its crumpled mass against a series of reef points higher up the sail

Rigging: all the rope used to control the masts and sails, that supporting the masts (shrouds, stays etc.) being known as standing rigging, and that controlling the sails (braces, sheets etc.) being known as running rigging

Rudder: surface hinged to the stern of a boat or ship to provide steering

Schooner: fast vessel fore-and-aft rigged on all its masts, but sometimes carrying square sails as well

Sheet: rope used to control the foot of a sail

Ship: properly speaking, a vessel with square sails on at least three masts

Shroud: rope used to brace the mast against side-to-side movement

Spanker: four-sided fore-and-aft sail attached to the mizzen mast

Spar: horizontal or angled length of wood to which the head of a sail is attached

Square-rigged mast: any mast with square sails

Stay: rope used to brace the mast against backward and forward movement

Staysail: triangular sail attached to a stay between the masts

Steering oar: long oar used to steer a boat or ship

Stempost: upright constructional member at the bow

Stern: back of a boat or ship

Sternpost: upright constructional member at the stern

Stringers: small timbers connecting the frame in a fore-and-aft direction

Tacking: sailing into the wind in a series of zigzags so that the wind comes from one side of the ship. The ship is then turned (tacked) so that the bow passes through the wind, which then hits the other side of the ship

Transom: a flat surface joining the sides of the boat or ship at the stern

Trimaran: boat in which three hulls (generally a large central unit with two smaller units outboard) are connected above the waterline

Tumblehome: any inward curve of the hull between the waterline and the deck

Yard: alternative name for spar

Index